Best behaviour

**starting points
for effective behaviour management**

**Peter Relf
Rod Hirst
Jan Richardson
Georgina Youdell**

Published by Network Educational Press Ltd
PO Box 635
Stafford
ST16 1BF

First published 1998; reprinted 2000
© Peter Relf, Rod Hirst, Jan Richardson & Georgina Youdell 1998

ISBN 1 85539 046 9

Peter Relf, Rod Hirst, Jan Richardson & Georgina Youdell
assert the moral right to be identified as the authors of this work

Series Editor - Professor Tim Brighouse
Edited by Jo Morrison
Designed by Peter Relf & Redesigns Neil Gordon of Init Publishing

Thanks
to the many teachers
who contributed ideas and good prcatice
to our oen teaching and
to the compilation of this book

Foreword

A teacher's task is much more ambitious than it used to be and demands a focus on the subtleties of teaching and learning and on the emerging knowledge of school improvement.

This is what this series is about.

Teaching can be a very lonely activity. The time honoured practice of a single teacher working alone in the classroom is still the norm; yet to operate alone is, in the end to become isolated and impoverished. This series addresses two issues - the need to focus on practical and useful ideas connected with teaching and learning and the wish thereby to provide some sort of an antidote to the loneliness of the long distance teacher who is daily berated by an anxious society.

Teachers flourish best when, in key stage teams or departments (or more rarely whole schools), their talk is predominantly about teaching and learning and where, unconnected with appraisal, they are privileged to observe each other teach; to plan and review their work together; and to practise the habit of learning from each other new teaching techniques. But how does this state of affairs arise? Is it to do with the way staffrooms are physically organised so that the wall bear testimony to interesting articles and in the corner there is a dedicated computer tuned to 'conferences' about SEN, school improvement, the teaching of English etc., and whether, in consequence, the teacher leaning over the shoulder of the enthusiastic IT colleagues sees the promise of interesting practice elsewhere? Has the primary school cracked it when it organises successive staff meetings in different classrooms and invites the 'host' teacher to start the meeting with a 15 minute exposition of their classroom organisation and management? Or is it the same staff sharing, on a rota basis, a slot on successive staff meeting agendas when each in turn reviews a new book they have used with their class? And what of the whole school which now uses 'active' and 'passive' concerts of carefully chosen music as part of their accelerated learning techniques?

It is of course well understood that even excellent teachers feel threatened when first they are observed. Hence the epidemic of trauma associated with OFSTED. The constant observation of the teacher in training seems like that of the learner driver. Once you have passed your test and can drive unaccompanied, you do. You often make lots of mistakes and sometimes get into bad habits. Woe betide, however, the back seat driver who tells you so. In the same way the new teacher quickly loses the habit of observing others and being observed. So how do we get a confident, mutual observation debate going? One school I know found a simple and therefore a brilliant solution. The Head of the History Department asked that a young colleague plan lessons for her, the Head of Department, to teach. This lesson she then taught and was observed by the young colleague. The subsequent discussion, in which the young teacher asked,

> *"Why did you divert the question and answer session I had planned?"*

and was answered by,

> *"Because I could see that I needed to arrest the attention of the group by the window with some hands-on role play, etc."*

lasted an hour and led to a once-a-term repeat discussion which, in the end, was adopted by the whole school. The whole school subsequently changed the pattern of its meetings to consolidate extended debate about teaching and learning. The two teachers claimed that because one planned and the other taught both were implicated but neither alone was responsible or felt 'got at'.

So there are practices which are both practical and more likely to make teaching a rewarding and successful activity. They can, as it were, increase the likelihood of a teacher surprising the pupils into understanding or doing something they did not think they could do rather than simply entertaining them or worse still occupying them. There are ways of helping teachers judge the best method of getting pupil expectation just ahead of self-esteem.

This series focuses on straightforward interventions which individual schools and teachers use to make life more rewarding for themselves and those they teach. Teachers deserve nothing less for they are the architects of tomorrow's society and society's ambition for what they achieve increases as each year passes.

Professor Tim Brighouse

Contents

Rationale

The behaviour management strategies in this resource are based on new information which has been learned about the brain in recent years. Some of this has direct implications for us as teachers, and explains some of those questions that have baffled us for years, like:

- I've explained that really carefully. Why haven't they understood?
- Why do they keep on talking when I've told them to stop?
- Why can't this pupil remember such a basic fact?
- Why do they get it right now and then fail later on?

In the following paragraphs is a very basic guide to what we know about the brain. A fuller explanation appears in *Accelerated Learning in the Classroom* by Alistair Smith (Network Educational Press ISBN: 1855390345).

The brain is actually in three parts:

The base, the oldest part, is called the reptilian brain. This governs our basic responses and survival instincts like fight and flight and territory.

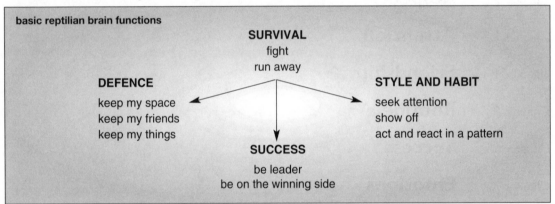

The mid brain is called the limbic system and governs emotion, values and memory. It also filters information to the top part of the brain if it sees it to be valuable.

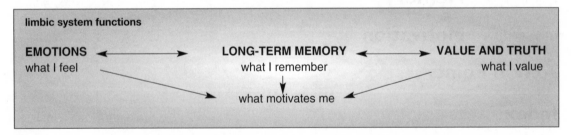

The top part of the brain (the 'walnut' we are familiar with) is called the neo-cortex. This governs the higher order thinking skills like language, logic, pattern recognition and imagination

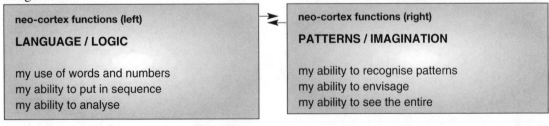

And here is what we now know. If the brain perceives its owner to be under threat, whether this threat is physical, emotional or indeed real, the blood supply retreats from the neo-cortex and the limbic system to fuel the reptilian brain. This is to enable it to protect its owner. When this happens, the other parts of the brain do not work effectively.

Let's assume that the threat is perceived to have gone. The blood supply resumes. Now we have to keep the limbic system happy. If the information this part of the brain is receiving does not match its owner's value system, it will not filter that information into the neo-cortex, or the memory. If its owner is not emotionally involved with the material, it will reject it.

So, when learners feel safe and successful, they are not in a state of stress, which would hinder or even prevent learning. When learners feel there is a value in what they are learning, when they are emotionally engaged, then they allow learning up into the neo-cortex, the thinking part of their brain.

As teachers, we are charged with developing pupils' skills, knowledge and concepts, which to a large degree involve the left-brain and right-brain functions of the neo-cortex. When pupils are under stress (for reasons inside and outside the classroom and the school), the neo-cortex part of their brain is not functioning at its best. Only when the needs of the other parts of the brain - the reptilian brain and the limbic system - are met, is learning able to take place more easily.

Pupils whose difficult behaviour is inhibiting their own learning and the learning of others are often under stress. They are likely to be preoccupied with the concerns of the reptilian brain and/or the limbic system. These parts of the brain pose demands unlike those of the neo-cortex. For example:

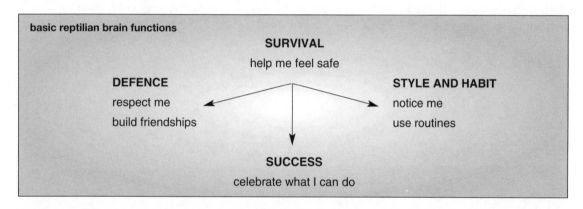

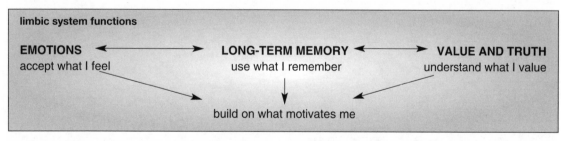

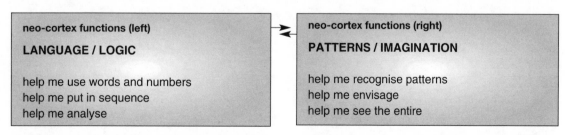

When we understand the differing nature and the priorities of these concerns and demands, we can use strategies to meet them so that difficult behaviour is minimised and learning is maximised.

The theory is straightforward, but reality is more complex. Our brains have the same functions as our pupils. It is all too easy when faced with difficult behaviour, for a teacher to feel stressed, to become emotional, defensive, perhaps even aggressive. Even if the downward rush of blood cannot be avoided, we need strategies that can be implemented even when we are under stress, so that we can lift ourselves and our pupils to a state where learning can take place.

Best behaviour shows strategies that can be used to keep the reptilian brain and the limbic system happy, so that we can maximise learning in our classroom. It looks at the agenda of the reptilian brain and the limbic system from a pupil perspective and then in terms of staff action. The *Best behaviour* strategies to promote good behaviour and learning are used by teachers widely and successfully. The companion booklet *Best behaviour FIRST AID* offers action points for handling challenging behaviour in the heat of the moment.

Behaviour management should not be a lonely struggle behind a closed classroom door. Consequently, *Best behaviour* also looks at staff development implications and whole school issues so that all members of the school community can play their part in promoting good behaviour and learning.

This resource offers starting points to promote a sense of security, respect, attention, friendship, routine and success. It explores also how emotions, values and memory all contribute to behaviour management.

A sense of security

CHAPTER 1 IN OUTLINE:

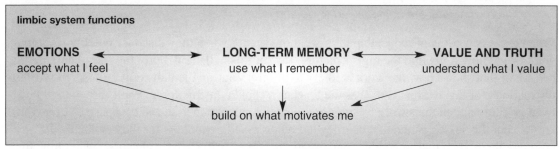

pupil perspectives

an organised start
a structure for the lesson
an organised finish
a code of conduct
coping with difficult situations

staff action

a safe classroom
a structured lesson
consistent expectations
coping with difficult situations

staff support action

what managers can do to support staff
what individual staff can do to support each other
how individuals can help themselves

whole school action

policy into practice
monitoring safety

A sense of security

an organised start

● *Pupils feel welcome and are used to a short
introductory routine that provides a settled start.*

Pupils are more secure when a lesson begins with a welcoming smile and positive comments about them that shows their teacher is interested in them as people. The sense of safety is even better when they have an established place to start the lesson and when they already know what to do straightaway. Although it is an organised start, it does not have to be stiff and starchy. They have learned what is expected of them and once the expectations were clear, they have talked through with their teacher how they could adapt the starting procedure to match the changing nature of their work. Above all, they know that when they start a lesson in this way, their attitude and readiness to get themselves organised for work is not taken for granted, but genuinely appreciated by their teacher.

a structure for the lesson

● *Pupils know quickly what a lesson has in store for them
and what they are being asked to do and learn.*

When today's work is introduced, pupils are more secure when they discover quickly what that work is and how it fits into the bigger picture, say, of this half-term's programme. There might be a chart that shows how the work is likely to progress during the half-term, or a set of written instructions for this lesson, as well as the teacher's spoken instructions. Pupils are not held up from getting on with their work by long or repeated explanations. In a short space of time, they know what this lesson is about, what they are being asked to do, how far they can make it uniquely theirs with their own ideas and creativity. They also have an idea how much time they have for particular activities. The lesson does not yawn ahead for them, but has a sequence of different shorter activities which make tolerable those parts they would rather not do.

 A journey on the London Underground fills many people with apprehension and a sense of insecurity. It is much less difficult when we have seen the map, know the general direction, eg: Eastbound, and how many stops there are before we reach our destination. Each lesson or series of lessons is preferably a new journey with purpose and staging points rather than another pointless circuit of the Circle Line.

an organised finish

● *A lesson comes to a close rather than a sudden stop
and pupils review the lesson with their teacher.*

Pupils feel safe when a lesson ends in an orderly way. It is reassuring when there is enough time to return equipment, to collect work and to tidy the area and when there is time to think back on what they have achieved. A short discussion on what caused concern or difficulty, and what was enjoyed and found to be interesting can shape work in subsequent lessons. When such discussion turns mistakes into learning points, promotes constructive criticism and inhibits fear of failure, pupils feel much more secure. A lesson ends well for pupils when their teacher expresses appreciation for what they have done during the lesson (and what they have considered in these closing stages) and when they can leave the teaching area quickly without being trampled underfoot.

A sense of security

a code of conduct

● *Pupils can see in the way that a code of conduct is upheld that it applies to all, for the safety of all.*

Pupils need to know not only where they stand with staff and with each other, but also to feel that their situation is safe - and safeguarded. A code of conduct which is expressed simply and which is applied and upheld consistently helps make school a more secure place for pupils. This is particularly so if they can see the code being applied to all people in school and if they themselves can turn to the code to safeguard themselves from threatening behaviour from other pupils or from staff.

coping with difficult situations

● *Pupils may share responsibility with staff for calm resolution of difficult situations.*

Pupils need to know that difficulties are resolved safely in school. Whatever their own role in a difficult situation, they want staff to stay as calm as humanly possible and to build a non-threatening sense of community in the classroom. This involves pupils having and exercising responsibilities as well as rights.

Most pupils enjoy having some responsibility. Pupils who experience difficulty in controlling emotion can value the ability to refer themselves to a support room or safe haven to ensure their own and others' safety. Pupils appreciate having some degree of choice not only in their work but in the heat of a difficult situation too where a genuine get-out can offer them a degree of control which is much safer for everybody than being backed into a corner.

A sense of security

a safe classroom

It is worth looking afresh at how well we use a room to promote a sense of security for pupils as well as for ourselves. We do not need to go into the furniture removal business in a big way, but we could think again about how flexible the arrangements might be so that we could expect pupils to work in different ways without a great upheaval. Each room we teach in has different snags and advantages. The following action points can help us work out more effective ways we can promote a sense of security in the way we use classrooms:

> ☞ Check where it is easiest for all pupils to notice, to see and hear us when we need to command their attention.
>
> ☞ Check how easy we can make it for pupils to get to and from resources or our help without disturbing others.
>
> ☞ Check if the front of the classroom is the best place for us to help and supervise pupils.
>
> ☞ Assess how little furniture needs to be moved to enable pupils to work in a different configuration and which pupils we are asking to move.
>
> ☞ Assess what scope there is for use of the back of a classroom for discreet supervision that does not threaten pupils, or the middle of the classroom for siting resources.
>
> ☞ Notice how some groupings and seating arrangements can be more conducive to some types of learning than others.

This way, we can establish patterns in how the classroom is to be used, with different places for different activities, for ourselves as well as our pupils. One way to underline these patterns of working to promote a sense of security is to express appreciation for positive ways pupils use the classroom and work in particular groupings.

 Architects survey the land, check communication routes and seek to meet clients' needs and safety standards before planning a building. We do the same when we plan lessons for the spaces architects have given us to work in.

a structured lesson

Everybody in the classroom feels more secure when lessons are well planned, with a clear purpose expressed as a learning outcome. We can take action for a well structured lesson in a variety of ways:

> ☞ Organise set places for pupils to start a lesson.
>
> ☞ Make a set pattern of work the normal way we start a lesson.
>
> ☞ Set up safe systems for pupils themselves to access equipment and resources with minimum fuss.
>
> ☞ Explain what we expect pupils to learn this lesson, not just what they will be doing.
>
> ☞ Make instructions short and straightforward.
>
> ☞ Indicate how long pupils have for a task or an activity.

A sense of Security

- ☛ Match task expectations to individual pupils' needs and capabilities.
- ☛ Build lessons with several short activities.
- ☛ Time the ending to enable work to be collected and the area left tidy.
- ☛ Make time for pupils to review with us good points and learning concerns from the lesson.

consistent expectations

Pupils feel more secure and we ourselves are on safer ground when all of us know and apply the standards the school expects of us and our pupils, for example from a code of conduct. It is worth checking how consistent we are.

- ☛ Expect the same standards of behaviour from lesson to lesson.
- ☛ Match our standards with those of the rest of the department or school.
- ☛ Express appreciation for standards achieved. We should not take it for granted.

coping with difficult situations

We need a few routine ways of coping with situations where normally we would feel vulnerable. Chapter 5, Routine, offers more ideas, and so too does *Best behaviour FIRST AID*.

- ☛ Ignore a provocation.
- ☛ Offer pupils a get-out, eg: 'What are you going to do about this?' or 'How can you improve this situation?'
- ☛ Make light of the situation and do not always seek to conquer.
- ☛ Keep the voice calm and volume low.
- ☛ Affirm the positive of the individual, of the group or class.
- ☛ Have help at hand from a supportive colleague.
- ☛ Team-teach.
- ☛ Arrange an exit procedure for a pupil.

Actors rehearse their lines, their tone of voice, their facial expression and their body language before going on stage. In the unfolding drama of a classroom, we can have a range of reactions available to us to promote a sense of security before we turn to other forms of action.

A sense of security

what managers can do to support staff

As managers we can build a sense of security for staff by clarifying regularly with each other and with them what values are being promoted (and how), what routines are being established (and how), what the boundaries are and what kinds of responses might be appropriate when boundaries are crossed. By building confidence in the implementation of school systems and procedures - especially for handling challenging behaviour - we make staff's work, and our own, easier.

As managers we can help colleagues feel secure in their teaching by having clear schemes of work which offer a range of learning activities that can be applied in differing circumstances. When we are alert to potential difficulties colleagues face and offer ideas on how to prevent them arising, then we are doing more still to build security. Achievable targets for each staff member needing behaviour management support can promote a sense of progress, success and confidence for the individuals and the department.

As managers we can also arrange behaviour management support during lessons, for example with a rapid response system that brings additional help to cope with an emergency, or with a safe haven for pupils or with team-teaching opportunities.

As managers we can arrange support for a teaching review where staff achievements in behaviour management are valued and appreciated and where staff self-esteem is promoted. Such a review can help colleagues recognise particular difficulties they and we face and consider afresh how they with their colleagues might adapt their approach to such difficulties.

 Health and Safety officers look for risk assessments and effective emergency procedures in the work-place. Managers and department colleagues can improve safety by assessing those parts of the curriculum where staff and pupils might feel less secure, set up measures to prevent hazards and establish emergency and escape procedures.

what individual staff can do to support each other

As colleagues we can promote a sense of security for pupils and ourselves by planning together a series of lessons which have activities and routines that foster a safe environment. We might agree to team-teach some lessons, with clear agreement about roles each or both of us will take.

Above all, we need to feel free to ask each other for help and to offer constructive assistance and advice when it is requested. We can listen to each other's concerns in a supportive way in order to:

- ☞ Clarify what factors are leading to a sense of insecurity.

- ☞ Gauge how far a sense of security has in fact been achieved already.

- ☞ See what help is available if it is needed.

 The Samaritans listen to callers and do not pass judgement on them. Colleagues need to feel accepted and valued especially when they feel unsafe in their teaching.

A sense of security

how individual staff can help themselves

As individuals we need to accept any sense of insecurity we may have. Like many other teachers we may feel anguish, frustration, despair, self-doubt and anger. It is best to off-load these emotions to someone who is ready to listen. As we do this, we can recognise that pupils' difficult behaviour may also be an expression of anguish, frustration, despair, self-doubt and anger. It is amazing how infectious these emotions can be.

One constructive method of handling our own sense of insecurity is for us to reflect in a cool, dispassionate and detached way on what has been contributing to that feeling. By re-playing an insecure scene in our minds we can:

- ☛ Spot how a sense of insecurity developed.
- ☛ Consider alternative ways of playing the scene.
- ☛ Identify what might have promoted a stronger sense of security.

That way we can develop a mental repertoire of positive ways to build a sense of safety for pupils and for ourselves. We can then try them out to assess their effectiveness. We do not always get things right first time.

A sense of security

policy into practice

As senior managers, we can review all school policies to see how well they set out clear values and ways to implement those values in order to promote a sense of security for all members of the school community. We need to clarify regularly with a cross-section of the school community:

- what values about safety and security are being promoted (and how)
- what routines for safety and security are being established (and how)
- what the boundaries are
- what kinds of responses might be appropriate when boundaries are crossed

We ensure that all of us as members of the school community have regular reminders of what we can do to foster a safe climate in school.

☛ Refer frequently, but not too frequently, to the code of conduct, for example in assemblies. Print it in pupil organisers, newsletters and other home contacts.

☛ Be alert to safety issues in school council meetings, teaching and/or non-teaching staff meetings and staff training days.

☛ Revise induction programmes for any new member of the school community so that a sense of security is established quickly.

☛ Display the Childline number. Provide pupils with easy access to a telephone.

monitoring safety

As senior managers we can check regularly the extent to which a sense of security is a feature of school life (from discussions, incident reports and other referrals):

- *which* pupils and staff feel safe / unsafe in school
- *when* pupils and staff feel safe / unsafe in school
- *where* pupils and staff feel safe / unsafe in school

Such information helps us assess what is promoting or hindering a sense of security for pupils and staff.

We need to use information from monitoring to:

☛ Clarify and refine policy.

☛ Modify existing systems and structures, for example:
  - speed up the handling of difficulties
  - improve communication with pupils, colleagues and people at home

☛ Set up new systems and structures, for example:
  - activities, quiet room, detention room, at breaks and lunchtime etc.,
  - safe havens for pupils under stress.

Respect

CHAPTER 2 IN OUTLINE:

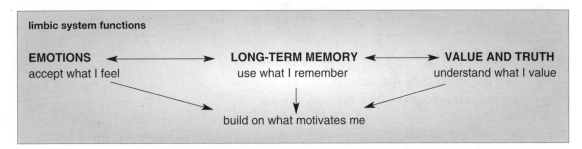

pupil perspectives

responsibilities and manners
active listening
recognition of pupil achievements

staff action

relationships
conducting lessons
respect when faced with difficult behaviour
image

staff support action

what managers can do to support staff
what individual staff can do to support each other
how individuals can help themselves

whole school action

responsibility
systems for respect
a culture of respect

Respect

responsibilities and manners

● *Pupils want us to give them respect in the ways we treat them, and share responsibility.*

Pupils want respect. They want us to treat them in a way that indicates we value them first as people and then as learners. Pupils evaluate our attitudes towards them just as we do with people in authority over us. Like us, they will be on the look-out for the simple things that we feel some superiors may be slow to give us: recognition, appreciation, responsibility, challenge and encouragement - you could add to the list. Like us, they will give respect to people who treat them well and think highly of them.

Some pupils may discover only when they are at school what it is like to be treated with respect, to earn respect and to give respect to other people. How we behave towards them is one of the quickest and most effective lessons we ever teach.

Some pupils may carry much heavier responsibilities outside school than we might give them inside school. Many pupils will gauge our respect for them by how far we keep responsibility to ourselves and how fairly we share responsibility.

active listening

● *One way of showing respect to pupils is to listen to them and understand their viewpoint.*

Pupils feel respected when we listen to their interests, their concerns and viewpoints. Active listening means that we give them time to speak and that we put to one side everything that we find pressing. The respect comes in giving them time, in understanding what they are saying, in putting ourselves in their shoes. It also comes in not delaying a conversation or discussion too long. What is urgent for them should not appear to be dismissed as unimportant by us.

Pupils who learn about respecting each other's ideas and concerns in a supportive way are capable of showing respect to each other, especially when they have opportunities to apply active listening themselves during lessons - in pairs, in groups or as a whole class.

recognition of pupil achievements

● *Pupils gain self-respect when they can see (and we notice) that they are making progress.*

Pupils know they are respected when we appreciate and recognise their efforts and we avoid adding a voice of criticism or patronising encouragement. They want short term targets which are achievable yet which are not insultingly easy. They need self-respect as well as respect from others. The way we review and record achievement and notice the progress they are making helps pupils gain self-respect.

Respect

relationships

We build respect for pupils and win respect for ourselves in the ways we relate to pupils. There are many straightforward ways to do this, for example:

- ☞ Be welcoming to all pupils, including those we might not be keen to see.
- ☞ Deal fairly with pupils.
- ☞ Be well-mannered with pupils.
- ☞ Give pupils personal space and time to carry out what we ask them to do.

conducting lessons

We demonstrate our respect for pupils by preparing lessons to meet pupils' learning needs rather than just to cover content. Respect is also evident in other ways we run our lessons:

- ☞ Mark assignments with care, legibly and with personalised comments.
- ☞ Return marked assignments on time.
- ☞ Keep pupils' work in set places in the classroom.
- ☞ Return written work, folders, books by hand and with care.
- ☞ Value what individuals or groups have done.
- ☞ Display pupils' work appropriately.

respect when faced with difficult behaviour

It is not easy to show respect for people whose behaviour we find irritating, annoying or unpleasant. The skill is in separating the difficult behaviour from the person and making it clear that it is the behaviour we are criticising. During a reprimand we may be faced with even more challenging behaviour but to add that to our criticism is to weaken our main case. As a result, we need to:

- ☞ Focus on the primary cause for criticism, not subsequent (secondary) behaviour(s).
- ☞ Explain the effect of behaviour on the person's own learning, the learning of other pupils, community relationships, whole school organisation, etc.
- ☞ Raise our voice only occasionally.

image

We need to be aware of how pupils assess the degree of respect we show to them in the clothes we wear, the way we move, where we stand or sit in a classroom, our facial expression, tone of voice, the tidiness of our classroom and so on.

Respect

what managers can do to support staff

As managers we can develop respect by discussing with colleagues what opportunities we provide that promote respect of pupils and of staff. We can clarify how courtesy and respect underpin the code of conduct and other school policies, for example: assessment. We need to become a positive role model, both in relationships with pupils and in relationships with our colleagues. When respect breaks down, we can trigger a team response in providing support and practical help.

As managers we can offer mentoring support to staff.

☞ Show empathy to staff facing difficulties.

☞ Give recognition to capabilities colleagues already have.

☞ Promote positive attitudes towards pupils whose behaviour is challenging.

☞ Use *Best behaviour* to focus on areas for support and possible action points.

☞ Consider which colleagues are best placed to provide mentoring and support.

what individual staff can do to support each other

As colleagues we can build the self-worth of others we work with by showing appreciation of their strengths, attitudes, skills and by being a supportive listener and critical friend for them. If possible, we can make opportunities to observe each other teach, focusing on the extent to which respect is evident in a lesson.

In staffroom discussions, we can promote constructive criticism of current systems for managing difficult behaviour. We build respect by focusing on strategies rather than personalities.

We should all be free to seek a colleague with whom there is mutual respect to act as a supportive listener and critical friend for us.

how individual staff can help themselves

We can use ideas from *Best behaviour*, but we do not have to rely entirely on our own efforts. We need to be ready to trust colleagues to support us in difficult situations and to accept their appreciation and constructive criticism.

Respect

responsibility

As senior managers we can show respect by making sure that existing groups (departments, key stage groups and so on) have real influence and responsibility. We can define line-management responsibilities for heads of department, subject co-ordinators and cross-curricular co-ordinators, but we also need to develop the capability of these people to carry out responsibilities in order to foster staff and pupil respect.

Mutual respect across the school community is well supported when a pupils' council, a teachers'/all-staff committee and the governing body can agree to tackle an issue of common concern and exert their particular influence and responsibility to improve a situation. For example, the transformation of part of a primary school's grounds into a wildlife conservation area by staff, parents and pupils not only improves the school facilities for everyone but does much to build mutual respect and shared interest.

systems for respect

We need to check that all teaching and non-teaching staff know and apply policies which concern respect for pupils and all other members of the school community. We can monitor the implementation and effectiveness of policies by:

- ☞ checking how incidents are being handled.

- ☞ noticing in conversations with pupils, staff and parents how different members of the school community relate to them.

- ☞ being involved with the PSE curriculum and developing it.

a culture of respect

There are many ways we can build a culture of respect throughout the school community. For example:

- ☞ seek to improve the ways the school acknowledges successes by all its members (not just pupils) whether in examinations, assessment, sport, creative arts, support for those in need, or other interests and activities.

- ☞ seek ideas for action that promote citizenship, a sense of community and voluntary service.

- ☞ be sensitive to how public or private our expression of appreciation might be.

- ☞ create opportunities for pupils and colleagues to be involved in the community through work experience, teacher placements, voluntary service and so on.

- ☞ champion opportunities for pupils and colleagues to be involved together as a community through residentials, camps, sports events, music and drama productions.

Attention

CHAPTER 3 IN OUTLINE:

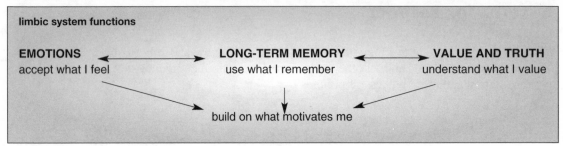

pupil perspectives

getting attention
attention focused on learning
rewards
coping with difficult situations

staff action

getting to know each other as individuals
attention focused on learning
rewards
setting and maintaining limits
giving support
giving responsibility to give and gain attention

staff support action

what managers can do to support staff
what individual staff can do to support each other
how individuals can help themselves

whole school action

openness
forums
equal opportunities

Attention

getting attention

● *Pupils like to be noticed and appreciated for who they are and what they do.*

Pupils are well practised from life at home, on the streets and in the playground on how to get attention and they are well aware of what the results of getting attention are. They want to be known and included by the adults and young people in their life. But even more, they want to be valued and appreciated for who they are and what they do. When they feel unnoticed by people they consider important, they are likely to make unwelcome efforts to be recognised as someone worth taking note of, someone to be reckoned with. As adults, we are pretty much the same.

attention focused on learning

● *Pupils give attention to their learning when they find it stimulating.*

Pupils naturally give attention to what is new and interesting. When a lesson has appropriate pace, interest and challenge, then they are more likely to give attention to learning. Not only is difficult behaviour reduced, but pupils are less inclined to give attention to it. When they know that their individual progress is being noticed and catered for - that we care about how well they are doing - they are again more likely to focus attention on learning.

rewards

● *Pupils value rewards which add to their sense of worth. The way the rewards are given can add or detract worth.*

Learners of all ages do like to know that their school, college or university notices and values their work and their attitude to work. A personalised reward - anything from an appreciative comment to an inscribed trophy - is a way of being seen as somebody of worth, particularly when an established standard is met or exceeded. If there is sensitivity to the degree of publicity given to a reward (from rejoicing in the streets to a one-to-one recognition) and an opportunity for people at home to know about their successes, then pupils continue to appreciate being given attention.

The rewards do not always have to be from us, the establishment. Pupils need opportunities in their school experiences to acknowledge and appreciate each other.

coping with difficult situations

● *Pupils value schools where challenging behaviour is handled discreetly.*

Most pupils prefer school life to be on an even keel where we help resolve difficulties in a calm, logical and private way, where we give attention either as unobtrusively as possible during lessons or we use other arenas / other times to give detailed attention. They want to know that we still value them as people even when we are criticising or punishing undesirable behaviour.

Attention

getting to know each other as individuals

Perhaps it is not so odd that we need to give attention to pupils as part of the deal that they give their attention to us. It means knowing them as people and revealing ourselves as real people to them. Pupils have a life outside school with experiences which can contribute to or hamper their learning and their relationships with us. When we know something of these experiences by giving them our attention we can gauge what line to take in gaining their attention.

- ☞ Be sociable with pupils. Give them time, eg: at end of lessons, around school, on duty.
- ☞ Use pupils' first names.
- ☞ Give pupils sustained attention when necessary, eg: breaks, lunchtime, after school.
- ☞ Listen to what pupils are really saying to us and do not jump to conclusions.
- ☞ Find ways to support and understand individual circumstances.
- ☞ Offer social opportunities outside the classroom, eg: clubs, activity weeks, 11th sessions.

attention focused on learning

It is all too easy for our own attention to be deflected from learning onto behaviour management. We need to find ways to explain quickly to pupils what we expect of them. This means having our own clear view of what the learning outcome is of a lesson or series of lessons and keeping attention on that goal.

- ☞ Clarify with pupils what they should be learning in each lesson.
- ☞ Share what the content is of the course or lesson and its demands and deadlines.
- ☞ Offer pupils scope for decisions in presentation, methods or work to be done.
- ☞ Give recognition to positives in pupil behaviour to divert or defuse the negatives.
- ☞ Get pupils' wandering attention back onto learning by focusing on the learning rather than any misbehaviour.
- ☞ Call a pupil's name, get eye contact, use gestures to signal a back-to-work message.
- ☞ Say a few words about the learning to change the focus from misbehaviour to work.

rewards

The school gives attention to pupils through its reward system. As a system it needs to be seen as consistent and fair. That has implications for us in how we operate it.

- ☞ Know what standards the school sets for rewarding pupils' good work and behaviour.
- ☞ Give recognition to individuals as well as groups.
- ☞ Accentuate the positive.
- ☞ Ensure that the school communicates success with home.

Attention

setting and maintaining limits

The school also gives attention to pupils through the implementation of its code of conduct. As with rewards, it is a system which we need to apply consistently and fairly in the way we give attention to difficult behaviour.

- ☛ Refer pupils to the expectations of the code of conduct.

- ☛ Give positive attention that encourages improved behaviour.

- ☛ Talk about the behaviour and criticise it rather than insult the person.

- ☛ Rebuke in a calm and logical way. Avoid giving to a pupil a peer-group audience.

giving support

The attention we give to pupils needs to be both positive and supportive - promoting good behaviour. It needs to reassure all concerned rather than become unwelcome intrusion. Procedures for pupils and parents to signal rising tension and difficulty, for pupils to seek help during a lesson or at any time during the school day, are examples of supportive strategies for pupils whose behaviour can be difficult. This kind of support is likely to need a blend of action and sensitivity.

- ☛ Meet pupil and parents to offer procedures that reduce unacceptable behaviour.

- ☛ Use pupil planners to set targets, small-steps action-points, to communicate success.

- ☛ Make positive enquiries about reasons for absence.

- ☛ Sense how to give attention with the least distraction to others.

- ☛ Recognise, without criticism or prejudice, the different living conditions pupils experience and share attention and support across the class.

- ☛ Create opportunities and space for pupils to work outside the classroom.

- ☛ Offer ourselves as mentors (and role models) to pupils.

- ☛ Be ready to back off when giving attention blurs into intrusion.

giving responsibility to give and gain attention

We do not have to keep all responsibility to ourselves for giving and gaining attention. We can delegate attention giving to pupils and offer learning styles where pupils have responsibility for keeping their attention on the work.

- ☛ Give responsibility to pupils via leadership roles, care for the classroom environment, school council, clubs and societies etc. Avoid favouritism.

- ☛ Offer choice and responsibility in method, presentation and style as soon as pupils are ready to exercise such choice and responsibility.

- ☛ Encourage young people to think for themselves.

Attention

what managers can do to support staff

As managers we can show leadership by giving supportive attention to staff colleagues and to pupils in a variety of ways, for example:

- ☞ Support training of staff to listen as counsellors, mentors, tutors.

- ☞ Encourage activities beyond the classroom where staff can give pupils attention, for example: clubs, societies, activity week, 11th session.

- ☞ Help pupils and parents feel known, at ease, valued for their contribution.

- ☞ Encourage open discussion in department meetings, for example: about giving positive attention, about focusing on behaviour rather than the person.

- ☞ Set up workshops to share ways of giving attention to reduce difficult behaviour.

what individuals can do to support each other

As colleagues we need to trust and respect each other enough to discuss attention-giving strategies. For example we can:

- ☞ Give each other attention - talk to each other in a friendly, positive way about giving and gaining attention.

- ☞ Include pupils in conversations with parents or with other staff.

- ☞ Act as an advocate for pupils with colleagues, eg: if the relationship is breaking down.

- ☞ Observe each other or team-teach to consider strategies on giving and gaining attention.

how individuals can help themselves

We need to recognise that all colleagues face difficult pupil behaviour at some stage. We should be ready to talk through with a colleague how best to give attention to pupils whose behaviour is causing particular difficulty. In our discussion, we have to accept that all pupils have a positive side (however hidden), that we should give those qualities attention as well and find opportunities to show appreciation of pupils accordingly. In other words, we can seek to take an interest in pupils inside and outside the classroom, take every opportunity to give attention to them and talk to them about themselves, their interests and their work.

Attention

openness

As senior managers we can create an environment where all members of the school community can be heard and understood, noticed and appreciated, can know what is going on and make a contribution. Ways we do this include:

- ☞ seeking advice from staff, pupil and parent representatives on aspects of policy.

- ☞ giving to staff the kind of attention we want them to give pupils.

- ☞ recognising staff achievements
- ☞ seeking and meeting staff training needs } eg: through an appraisal system.

forums

We can involve teaching and non-teaching staff, pupils and parents in some aspects of the running of the school. For example, we might link formally our parent-governors and the parent-teacher association to enable a broad parental view to inform school management decisions. Similarly we might link governors from business with a local education-business partnership to enable a broad business view to inform our management decisions.

Many schools enable a pupil council to make recommendations to senior managers and governors. Some schools are now consulting non-teaching staff more frequently, keeping them informed of decisions and involving them in discussions and/or staff training days where appropriate.

However, no talking shop is worth having unless it can be *seen* to make a difference.

equal opportunities

As senior managers we ensure that all departments and subject co-ordinators promote equal opportunities. Examples of action include:

- ☞ Agree and monitor targets for further development of differentiation.

- ☞ Provide fair time-tabling, rooming and staffing which help staff and pupils give and gain attention as easily as possible.

- ☞ Agree and monitor targets for course content, demands and deployment of resources so that learning becomes more inviting.

- ☞ Offer mentoring schemes for students who have behavioural difficulties and for staff who have difficulty relating to and dealing with certain pupils.

- ☞ Check how far rewards and sanctions systems encourage attention-giving for positive reasons, for example, by emphasising improvement, by building self-worth of pupils and staff, by supporting positive relationships.

Friendship

CHAPTER 4 IN OUTLINE:

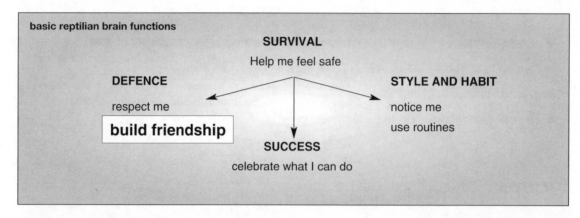

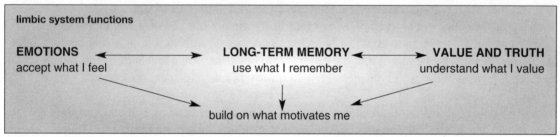

pupil perspectives

a friendly welcome
with a little help from my friends
we're all human
how am I doing?

staff action

return match
the same species
customer feedback
relaxed learning

staff support action

what managers can do to support staff
what individual staff can do to support each other
how individuals can help themselves

whole school action

good relationships
a buddy system
sensitive groupings

Friendship

a friendly welcome

● *Pupils value being greeted at the start of a lesson.*

Pupils sense how pleased we are to see them. Most of them want to be greeted. Many are ready to be friendly in return. The atmosphere can be warm and businesslike from the word go.

with a little help from my friends

● *Carefully planned groupings can help pupils work together well.*

Pupils like to work in groups, as teams. As a way of working it helps them affirm existing friendships and it can widen a network of friends too. It enables them to help each other in a learning task, to identify needs and to access our help more easily. If we give careful consideration to group dynamics, pupil groups themselves can promote good behaviour and can inhibit potentially difficult behaviour.

we're all human

● *Pupils are often good at assessing others. They can learn how to understand and accept others too.*

Pupils are quick to recognise each other's strengths and weaknesses and ours too. Instinct might lead them to apply the laws of the jungle. But with us they can learn more constructive ways of accepting a common humanity where they face and understand their own behaviour, other pupils' behaviour and our behaviour too.

how am I doing?

● *Pupils' self-worth is affected by the way we assess them as people and as learners.*

Pupils assess their own performance all the time and use it to adjust their sense of self-worth, perhaps over-estimating or under-estimating themselves. Whichever way, we need to handle their ego with care. Together, in a friendly way, they and we can negotiate targets and action points, and we learn how to feed back assessment in a constructive way.

Friendship

return match

Friendship, disinterest and animosity are contagious. Other people usually reflect back to us the attitudes we show them. So a friendly classroom atmosphere is likely to reduce the incidence of challenging behaviour. We know well enough how to be friendly!

- ☞ Display body language which gives positive messages, eg: a smile, arms unfolded.
- ☞ Talk in a friendly manner and use a friendly tone of voice with pupils.
- ☞ Remember what pupils have talked with us about previously.
- ☞ Say a genuine 'please' and 'thank you' to pupils. Be sincere and professional.

the same species

We need to recognise that we share human frailty with our pupils, which includes the possibility that we might not always be in the right and not always on the moral high ground.

- ☞ Accept that we may be wrong/mistaken.
- ☞ Freely admit to pupils that we are not perfect or omniscient.
- ☞ Accept that we may be at fault with pupils who are exhibiting behavioural difficulties.
- ☞ Be ready to apologise for our own behaviour as a gesture of friendship.

customer feedback

A simple way of showing friendship in the classroom is by encouraging dialogue about the learning process. From time to time we can ask for feedback from pupils, for example by providing room for pupil comment on an assessment form about how difficult or interesting they found an assignment. When we seek oral feedback - on a series of lessons or on another group's activity - we can weight the response, eg: two positive comments for every negative comment.

Successful companies do not assume that they know best and that their customers will get what is good for them. Instead, they are genuinely interested in customers' perceptions of the products they make. They befriend their customers, listen to feedback from them, consider what needs are not being met and improve their products accordingly.

relaxed learning

At an early stage in a new topic we can promote learning by adopting a friendly, relaxed approach which sees any learning problem a pupil has as *our* problem rather than *theirs*. This approach puts pupils at their ease, minimises potential sense of failure and gives us a coaching role where we take on the initial job of removing obstacles for them. Gradually as they grow in confidence, we can enable them to remove obstacles for themselves.

Friendship

what managers can do to support staff

As managers, we aim to promote a friendly atmosphere where staff can discuss problems about pupils displaying difficult behaviour in school. Ways we can achieve this include:

- ☛ Ensure that positive discussion about difficult pupils is on the agenda of departmental, year group and Key Stage meetings.

- ☛ Make time to listen to staff in a supportive way and offer advice.

- ☛ Include guidance on appropriate ways to handle difficult behaviour in staff and departmental handbooks.

- ☛ Set an example by taking an interest in staff and pupils.

- ☛ Help staff in a friendly rather than critical way to handle difficult behaviour.

- ☛ Promote and support staff social events which help create a friendly ethos in the school.

- ☛ Check that our advice to and demands of colleagues reflect our own behaviour.

what individual staff can do to support each other

As colleagues we need to listen to each other's problems in a non-judgemental way. Through friendly support and advice we encourage each other to clarify the nature of the problem, to explore ways of overcoming the problem and to arrange support if it is needed.

We should feel free to ask each other for help and advice without appearing to be less than competent. As colleagues we should also be ready to offer constructive help and advice when it is requested.

how individuals can help themselves

We help ourselves best by finding ways to relax in difficult situations. Then we can show body language, tone of voice and choice of language that build rapport.

Although it is a natural defence mechanism, we need to avoid stereotyping pupils or colleagues in ways which harm our relationship with them. Instead, we have to separate the challenging behaviour from the person, for example, saying "I don't like what you are doing" rather than "You are a pain in the neck." 'I' messages such as the former are astonishingly effective, whether in the classroom or the staffroom. When we use them, we help to manage behaviour effectively and to regain a positive climate. More examples of 'I' messages appear in *Best behaviour FIRST AID*.

As individuals we need to accept that all teachers face problems with pupils displaying challenging behaviour and that such problems should not be viewed with a sense of personal or unique failure. We need to listen to colleagues and pupils and be ready to accept advice and support perhaps from informal, self-support groups. It is not a sign of weakness to ask for advice from a colleague.

Friendship

good relationships

As senior managers we can check how far school policies promote friendly interaction, politeness and concern among all members of the school community. Likewise, it is useful to cast fresh eyes over school events and communications to see how well we use opportunities like those listed below to reinforce a genuine, friendly approach:

☞ assemblies, school council meetings, staff meetings.

☞ induction programmes for any new member of the school community.

☞ staff training days.

☞ references in newsletters and other home and community contacts.

☞ references in organiser diaries, records of achievement.

☞ the staff handbook.

It can be illuminating to ask new staff, pupils, parents and guests about their reception, for example:

- how easy it is to find reception;
- first impressions of the reception area;
- how friendly a welcome they receive.

This is all part of a process of monitoring regularly with a cross-section of the school community how well a friendly atmosphere is being built and sustained. Analysis of what is promoting or hindering friendly behaviour informs subsequent decisions and actions.

a buddy system

An increasing number of universities, schools and businesses now offer a 'buddy system'. In schools, the system enables new pupils and pupils facing particular difficulties to receive at least short-term support from other pupils. Befriending and reassurance make it easier for many pupils to settle to learning.

sensitive groupings

As managers, we place pupils into tutor groups sensitively so that existing friendship circles (from feeder schools, uniformed organisations, youth club, etc.) are not entirely lost. We can encourage classroom teachers to place pupils into a variety of groups for different learning tasks so that existing friendship circles can be sustained.

Routine

CHAPTER 4 IN OUTLINE:

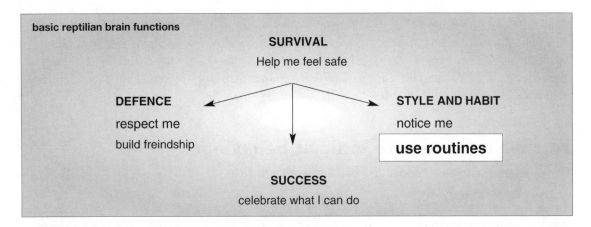

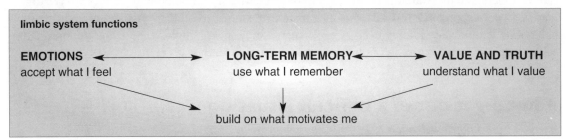

pupil perspectives

positive routine
routine responses to difficult behaviour
how to get out of a difficult situation

staff action

teaching routines
routine to prepare for learning
routine for consistency
routine for managing difficult behaviour

staff support action

what managers can do to support staff
what individual staff can do to support each other
how individuals can help themselves

whole school action

consistent approaches to difficult behaviour

Routine

positive routine

- *Pupils like routine and quickly learn new routines they recognise as essential or useful.*

Pupils appreciate knowing what they are expected to do at the start of a lesson, during it and at the end of it - as outlined in Chapter 1, A sense of security.

They are quick to learn routines that are patently necessary and that we insist on. For example they can and do learn how to access equipment and resources safely, without fuss, without having to ask. They can and do learn how to move from one activity to another safely, quickly and quietly. They can and do learn how to finish (rather than stop) by returning equipment and resources, by reviewing their work, by collecting work.

routine responses to difficult behaviour

- *Some pupils will need to learn low-key responses to challenging behaviour.*

Pupils understand there are different ways to respond to difficult behaviour, but they have to learn how to respond in a low key way as a matter of routine to other pupils showing difficult behaviour. Some may quickly become well-versed in ignoring, deflecting, using humour, using school support systems and so on, but others may need to learn such tactics as routines.

how to get out of a difficult situation

- *Some pupils will need to learn to read their own behaviour and how to keep self-control.*

Likewise, pupils whose behaviour is difficult can learn routine ways to handle their difficulties, for example: by counting to ten before responding, by breathing deeply, by self-referral to a safe haven and by use of other support systems in the school.

Lorry drivers learn as routine the driving skills they need to keep themselves, their vehicles, the goods they are transporting and other road-users safe. In some circumstances these routine skills are not enough. For example, a downhill lane of a steep hill may have a gravel-filled emergency escape lay-by which prevents vehicles whose brakes have failed from causing serious accidents. They are well-signed in advance so that drivers know they can be helped to get out of a difficult situation.

Routine

teaching routines

We need to use routine in moderation if we are to avoid teaching predictable, monotonous lessons. Instead, we use routine to help the smooth running and completion of a lesson. This way, we spend less time on classroom management and more time on learning. It leaves us free to stimulate interest in learning itself by our use of a variety of approaches.

- ☛ Create, teach and maintain routines appropriate for our teaching area, eg: coats off, equipment ready, bags away, starting places, constant initial task.

- ☛ Explain what is expected of pupils at the start of a year, term, module, topic, lesson.

- ☛ Prepare pupils for activities with routines for working: individually, in groups, as a class.

- ☛ Ensure pupils know routine procedures to carry out a task before we start a topic.

routine to prepare for learning

A key use of routine is to prepare pupils for their learning. In a routine introduction we can use the spoken and written word and diagrams to clarify quickly what we expect of pupils in a lesson.

- ☛ Indicate what skills, concepts, knowledge we expect pupils to learn, eg: on a notice as well as verbal instructions.

- ☛ Outline the tasks we are asking them to do, eg: on task cards as well as verbal instructions.

- ☛ Specify how achievement will be assessed and recognised, eg: on an assignment sheet as well as verbal instructions.

routine for consistency

Routines help us to be consistent from one lesson to the next, for example in treating each pupil / group / class fairly. A routine which has a clear rationale - set by the whole school, or agreed by our department - is easier to apply simply because of its consistency beyond our classroom. However, any routine needs to be reinforced (by praise, reminders, insistence) to promote constant expectations.

routine for managing difficult behaviour

We need routines to help us respond to difficult behaviour in a low-key way initially. That way we can set for ourselves a long ladder of responses to difficult behaviour (starting with lower rungs of raised eyebrows, stern look, quiet firm voice) which gives us and our pupils room for manoeuvre. *Best behaviour FIRST AID* offers routine ways of managing difficult behaviour.

Routine

what managers can do to support staff

As managers, we create with our departments routines that overcome difficulties in classroom management for example in collecting equipment and work, or in assessing practical work. We monitor the way we as a department use routines in lessons.

As a matter of routine, we consider behaviour management in department meetings.

what individual staff can do to support each other

As colleagues, we provide support routinely to each other, particularly before and after difficult lessons. With colleagues, we consider how far routine can help reduce difficult behaviour. See also Chapter 1, A sense of security and *Best behaviour FIRST AID*. We develop routine procedures for reflecting on lessons which encourage us to be objective and positive about each other and about pupils who show difficult behaviour.

how individual staff can help themselves

- ☛ Learn to respond to difficult behaviour as a matter of routine in a low-key way initially.

- ☛ Practise the range of responses to difficult behaviour which give us and our pupils room for manoeuvre.

- ☛ Plan routines to reduce stress levels before the next lesson with this class

- ☛ Plan and carry out routines that divert attention or return to learning objectives to deflect behaviour which challenges us personally.

Politicians who face both political attack and personal insult have become skilled in the art of deflection so that they can avoid or minimise self-doubt and individual isolation.

Routine

consistent approaches to difficult behaviour

As senior managers, we help all school staff (teaching and non-teaching) to know and apply policies concerning behaviour as a matter of routine. We ensure that school policies establish routine procedures for handling difficult behaviour. We monitor the implementation of these routine procedures.

Success
CHAPTER 6 IN OUTLINE:

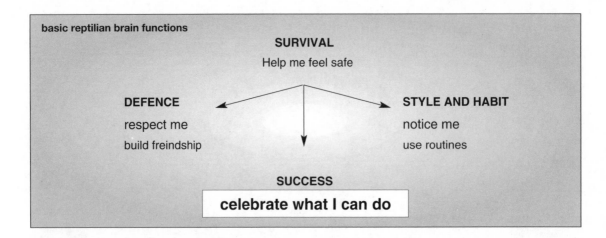

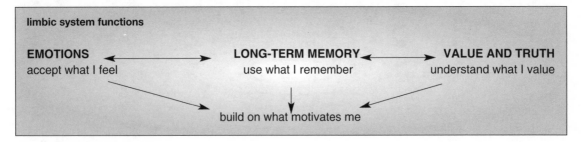

pupil perspectives
recognition
learning and achievement

staff action
commitment
coaching

staff support action
what managers can do to support staff
what individual staff can do to support each other
how individuals can help themselves

whole school action
career development programme
appraisal
public relations

Success

recognition

- *Pupils need to be told how much we value them and why.*
  They don't want to feel that they are being jollied along.

Pupils do not always know how much they are appreciated by us, by other pupils, by people at home and in the wider world. They need their qualities and achievements to be stated before they can feel recognised and valued. Those who have a lower sense of self-worth may need some convincing that the recognition is deserved and is not merely a ploy to encourage future achievement.

Like us, pupils like to work in a climate where their achievements and successes are celebrated and where apathy and failure are not met with blame but rather analysed and tackled in a supportive way.

learning and achievement

- *Pupils want to feel successful now and see how future*
  success is within their grasp.

Pupils do not always see the relevance of what we are asking them to do. When we know pupils as learners, when we discuss with them their learning needs and provide appropriate opportunities to meet their needs, then pupils can appreciate that what they are learning and how they are learning do have relevance to their development.

When pupils feel successful in some aspects of their work, they are more ready to accept without a sense of shame that other aspects of their learning need further attention. It is easier still when we clarify with them what steps they can take to achieve improvement. This is when pupils actively want achievable short-term targets with a plan of action - so that success is not a distant hope but a likely possibility, perhaps even this lesson!

Some pupils find it natural to reflect on how they have achieved success. But it is only when we prompt reflection and review in our feedback and encouragement that most pupils will understand how their past efforts have contributed to current success.

 Taking a horse to water is helpful when it is ready to drink. The rider gauges when the horse is likely to be thirsty but does not give up providing watering places when it chooses not to drink. Horses can die in deserts. But champion horses are bred in deserts too...

Success

commitment

If we want pupils to be committed to their learning, we need to show our commitment to them as people and learners. That means that we need to communicate to them that we know how well they are doing, that we understand what their strengths and their needs are and that we are deliberately using a variety of approaches to help overcome their difficulties. Pupils do not always understand that we are working in ways to help them succeed.

coaching

One of the ways of helping pupils succeed is to adopt a coaching approach where we not only know our subject thoroughly, but we understand the kinds of blockages to success that our pupils encounter. We can demonstrate to pupils our skills in both these areas in actions like the following:

☛ Accept initially our total responsibility for pupils' learning.

☛ Gauge our levels of direction and personal interaction to pupils' current capacity to tackle a learning task.

☛ Build pupils' self-respect by celebrating and recording their achievements and successes.

☛ Analyse difficulty and failure - and provide appropriate support.

☛ Set or agree challenges and goals at appropriate development points.

A chocolate bar as a reward for good work may motivate success once in a while, but not on a regular basis. The coaching teacher's belief in the learner ("You can achieve") is the best motivator.

Success

what managers can do to support staff

As managers, we foster success by showing interest in and having knowledge of what our staff colleagues are doing and how well they are doing it. Colleagues want us to recognise and value their commitment, their strengths and successes. It is all too easy when tackling the difficulties that schools generate each day to let the successes go unacknowledged.

We can help staff colleagues share successful practice, for example by discussing in our department a variety of ways to teach particular topics. This kind of support for members of the department who feel less confident is all part of a personal and professional development programme that encourages success and a sense of self-worth.

what individual staff can do to support each other

Each of us needs to notice and appreciate each other's commitment, strengths and successes. Familiarity can breed oversight. We can encourage success together in several ways:

- Plan work together.
- Team-teach.
- Share a workload.
- Play to each other's strengths.
- Share good practice.
- Discuss issues with colleagues.

how individuals can help themselves

To get a sense of success, we have to take a positive view of ourselves, our pupils and our colleagues. Certainly, we need to avoid a destructive, negative spiral in staff room conversations.

In the short term, we can notice our own successes more easily if we have a 'to-do' list (with priorities) to focus our work and to give us a sense of achievement as we tick off the tasks. In the longer-term, our sense of personal success is helped when we have a career development plan, preferably negotiated with our line-manager.

Success

career development programme

As senior managers we may not have much scope to reward staff for their successes. On the other hand, a career development programme can help recognise success and offer opportunities for new skills and experience. Career development is a form of personal and professional development which releases, exchanges and reshapes roles, responsibilities and tasks in order to enrich individual skills and to bring fresh perspectives to management.

appraisal

Staff involvement in an appraisal scheme is an important opportunity to identify the strengths and celebrate the successes our staff bring to school life. A personal and professional development programme linked to appraisal and the school development plan needs to be seen to develop existing strengths and to broaden horizons as well as to meet needs.

public relations

There is much we can do to help the school community view itself positively and note its success.

- ☞ Publicise achievement in school, in communications to pupils' homes, in press statements and photo opportunities.

- ☞ Emphasise to pupils, teachers and parents how the curriculum successfully serves life in the wider world, for example: through visits to industry and the community, through work experience related to one or more curriculum area[s], through adults other than teachers bringing their experience to the curriculum.

- ☞ Give recognition to successes in extra-curricular activities: sports, music, arts, drama and dance, uniformed organisations, Duke of Edinburgh Award scheme etc.

Emotions
CHAPTER 7 IN OUTLINE:

Now that the needs of the basic reptilian brain have been addressed, the remaining chapters of *Best behaviour* consider the concerns of the limbic system.

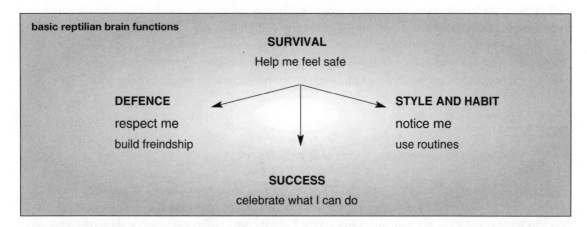

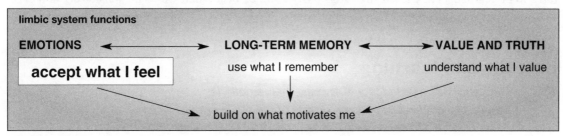

pupil perspectives
showing emotion is OK
but...
emotions in learning

staff action
valves to let off steam
avoiding 'undisciplined squads of emotion'

staff support action
what managers can do to support staff
what individual staff can do to support each other
how individuals can help themselves

whole school action
systems to release tension
organisational emotions

Emotions

showing emotion is OK

- *Pupils need to give vent to their feelings. They need to be heard and understood.*

Many pupils need opportunities to express their feelings. It is too much to keep them bottled up. The longer the pressure builds, the more likely pupils will be hurtful, obscene or offensive to others. So pupils need regular times and places - during lessons and during the school day - when they are able to express emotions to each other and to staff without causing offence. But to off-load their feelings at appropriate (not always planned) occasions pupils need someone else to hear, understand and share their emotion. It may be that we are the people to receive expressions of emotion, but some pupils can be very skilled in this too.

Some pupils do not understand that we have emotions just as they do. Others are skilled at playing on our emotions: winding us up, playing to the gallery or tugging at the heart-strings.

but . . .

- *Pupils need to learn when and how to express emotion.*

Pupils do not necessarily understand that there are some occasions when it is not appropriate to show their true feelings. They may not know how to control emotions on those occasions. Both have to be learned. They learn such sensitivity from us best when we teach sensitively and act in a sensitive way ourselves.

emotions in learning

- *How pupils acknowledge and engage their emotional responses to stimuli affects the quality of their learning.*

All learners' emotions are inextricably linked with memories. This is not surprising, as the limbic system is the seat of both. Many words evoke emotion. For example, the word 'mother' may prompt a sense of live or loss or anger, perhaps a smell or a feeling. Whatever the reaction, it is an emotional one. When pupils use words (and other features of the five senses) in their learning, there is scope for them to acknowledge their emotional response and to use emotions to enrich and strengthen their learning.

Emotions

valves to let off steam

Some pupils may find it difficult to loosen the stiff upper lip or not to keep their feelings to themselves. Others may need to discover how to reveal what they feel without making a situation worse. Our emotional state influences strongly the way we behave and our capacity to learn. As teachers we can provide frequent outlets that allow emotional pressure pupils may be feeling to be released without causing a scene. Also, we can model ways of handling emotion:

☞ Defuse a situation by using humour, by laughing at ourselves.

☞ Respond slowly with controlled expression of our own feeling, eg:
"'I'm too cross to talk about this now."

☞ Help pupils control their anger against themselves and against others.

☞ Use facial expression, gestures, body language to calm a distressed, disturbed pupil.

☞ Allow pupils to 'off-load' and get problems out of their system in a calm and supportive way in an appropriate place or time.

☞ Listen in a non-threatening way to pupils voicing their feelings.

avoiding 'undisciplined squads of emotion' *TS Eliot*

Just like our pupils, our own emotional state influences strongly the way we behave. When we are modelling ways of handling emotion we must be ready to accept our own feelings and be ready to declare our own emotions to pupils, eg:

"I feel uncomfortable / annoyed / ashamed / angry that..."
"I am delighted / amused by / looking forward to..."
"I am sorry, I apologise..."

With these kinds of words we can express our own feelings to pupils in a managed way that is not offensive, hurtful, personal or obscene to them. We are less likely to convey fear or a lack of control when we describe almost as an outsider what we are feeling inside. This is an extension of the technique of separating the behaviour from the person. Now there is scope for us to be critical of the behaviour and to describe an emotional response that the behaviour is causing. Pupils need to see that we have emotions and that we can control them.

Emotions

what managers can do to support staff

As managers, we are constantly addressing not only our own feelings but those of staff and pupils around us. It is important that staff see us as providing appropriate opportunities for them to express in a professional way their emotions about their work with pupils, with colleagues and with us. We need to recognise that our own behaviour and actions may be the cause of strong feelings. Hence our need to listen to and watch for feedback from staff and pupils.

We show that we do listen to and reflect upon staff concerns carefully, for example when we take action where appropriate and acknowledge its origins or when we subsequently explain why some action has not been appropriate or possible.

what individual staff can do to support each other

As colleagues, we need to listen to and show understanding for each other other's feelings. It is good to talk through situations with each other. When we are aware of another colleague's frustration, anger or low self-esteem, someone needs to offer a listening ear, to build confidence and where appropriate, to offer practical help. The listening alone may be enough.

For us, the staff room needs to be a safe haven where we show tolerance to each other and where we are ready to apologise.

how individual staff can help themselves

As individual teachers, we need to recognise that there are acceptable (and unacceptable) ways and times to express feelings to pupils and to colleagues.

Especially, we need to accept that we are not alone in facing behavioural difficulties. No one is perfect in handling difficult situations and our own attempts do have some merit. Expression of our emotions is not necessarily a sign of weakness.

Emotions

systems to release tension

An open-door policy is the easiest way we as senior managers can help keep in hand emotions across the school. When it is easy for any member of the school community to talk to us with little or no screening we are already helping to release tension. We then build a reputation for listening attentively and sympathetically and for being seen to act when appropriate.

In some schools, a suggestions box is a successful way of enabling all members of the school community to express feelings about and offer ideas on how to improve present circumstances. It is made clear that suggestions are read, and that all positive ideas are considered by relevant members of the school community. Where appropriate, positive ideas are translated into action. A suggestions box is used widely in industry to promote quality and improve efficiency.

organisational emotions

As senior managers, we can help the school use assemblies, special events, the arts, etc. to express emotions for example:

☛ pride and joy, eg: in achievements.

☛ sorrow and compassion, eg: in community service, in charity-giving, in sharing bereavement and grief.

☛ solidarity and friendship, eg: in European links.

☛ an emotion as a theme in an art exhibition, a musical / dance / drama event.

Values

CHAPTER 8 IN OUTLINE:

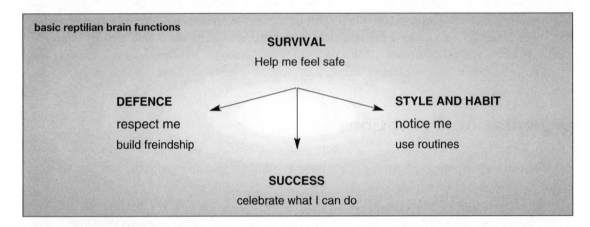

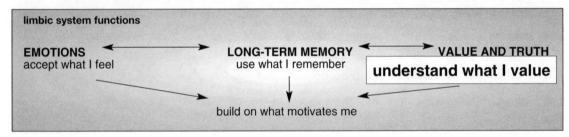

pupil perspectives

esteem
vive la difference
learning and behaviour

staff action

common ground
admitting bias
applying the code of conduct
handling pupil opinion-leaders

staff support action

what managers can do to support staff
what individual staff can do to support each other
how individuals can help themselves

whole school action

clear from the start
developing policies and practice

Values

esteem

- *Pupils put a value on themselves. If we question it, they want our fairness, not our preferences and prejudices.*

During their school life, pupils discover that they are unique. They place a value on themselves as people, as members of a family, of a [school] community and check out that assessment with the way other people value them. It is difficult to accept when significant people in their life think worse or better of them than they do.

They place a value on each other - often quite quickly in their social life - and are not always ready to suspend that assessment when evaluating each other's work. Explaining a valuation may expose underlying (perhaps unquestioned) preferences and prejudices. Despite this, they want to be recognised and appreciated by members of the school community, including us, and expect us to use our interactions with them to reconsider our preferences and prejudices and to adjust our assessment of them as people and learners.

vive la différence

- *Pupils may have limited exposure to different perspectives and how to use them to reappraise their own.*

Pupils need appropriate opportunities to express their opinions and values in lessons. They need to feel secure enough with each other and with us to express and discuss their social, educational, religious and cultural values, attitudes and beliefs. They learn to accept that other people have different values which might prompt them to reconsider some of their own values. Pupils need to meet and learn from people in the wider community

learning and behaviour

- *Pupils do not automatically see that what they learn in school links to society's expectations for their behaviour.*

Pupils may not notice immediate links between educational values and social behaviour. For example, the valuing of equal opportunities linked to the fall of apartheid and the need to avoid racist behaviour in school, in society; or the valuing of literacy and numeracy linked to adult education programmes and the need for lifelong learning. Pupils need to review and reconsider what they and others value about learning and relationships.

Values

common ground

During their school life, pupils are forming their opinions and values - at first reflecting the values from home, but also discovering and comparing, defending and challenging different values from other people (including us). They need appropriate opportunities to express their opinions and values in lessons as part of that formation process. We too need to understand and appreciate pupils' values and to find common ground with them.

☛ Reinforce shared values.

☛ Take care whether to ignore other values, or to explain why such values are difficult to accept.

☛ Never ridicule a pupil's opinion or values.

☛ Use group activities and class discussion to build rapport, trust, mutual respect and confidence in expressing and reconsidering values.

☛ Broaden our response to pupil values, eg: using a pupil's value of 'toughness' to prompt achievement of a tough, imminent deadline.

admitting bias

As part of pupils' values formation process we should be prepared to acknowledge to pupils how our own views and values may affect our attempt to present a topic in a neutral way or our degree of tolerance towards some kinds of behaviour.

applying the code of conduct

We express school values when we reinforce and show appreciation for behaviour in accord with the code of conduct. School values are not easy to change, but we should still be alert to pupil responses and act upon feedback pupils give about values in the code of conduct.

handling pupil opinion-leaders

We also need to be alert to prevalent pupil values in the classroom. We should know which pupils lead the opinions of others and assess the attitudes and values of these pupils, for example in terms of how sympathetic or antagonistic they are to the school's values. We need to check how far their influence extends currently and consider strategies to reinforce school values and defuse antagonism.

Values

what managers can do to support staff

From time to time, it is worth checking with our colleagues in a department how whole-school values apply to and affect the curriculum and how we manage behaviour. If we reveal discrepancies in the understanding and the application of values then we can find solutions and provide support that strengthen both curriculum delivery and behaviour management.

We need to prize open-mindedness and flexibility in this exercise. Our colleagues may use different approaches in the way they implement whole-school values and yet still achieve consistent application.

what individual staff can do to support each other

We all need to accept that colleagues may use different approaches in the way they implement whole-school values. As colleagues we should be ready to discuss opinions, approaches and attitudes to find common ground and to explore ways we can apply whole-school values more consistently.

how individual staff can help themselves

As individuals we need to be ready to adjust our opinions, approaches and attitudes in the light of discussions with colleagues about whole-school values. Also, we need to be honest with ourselves about our own values.

Values

clear from the start

As senior managers, we need to express whole-school values simply and publish them in school brochures and other induction literature. Whole-school values and their implications for learning and behaviour need to be explained to all new pupils, parents, staff and governors.

developing policies and practice

Values for learning and for behaviour are seen to be whole-school values when they are agreed by pupils, teaching and non-teaching staff, managers and governors. Because of a school's ever-changing population, a regular update (perhaps every three or four years) enables all members of the school community to contribute to and exercise collective responsibility for whole-school values.

Our review of school policies could identify a few relevant, simple-to-collect indicators of school values so that the practical application of whole-school values can be measured and monitored.

For values to be appreciated by members of the school community, there needs to be regular recognition (in assemblies, in tutor-time, on public occasions) of positive examples from school life of the practical application of whole-school values.

Memory

CHAPTER 9 IN OUTLINE:

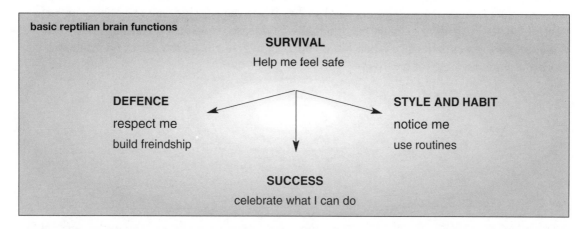

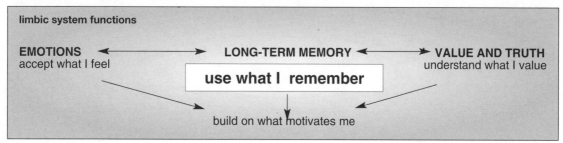

pupil perspectives

long-term memory

staff action

building long-term memory

staff support action

what managers can do to support staff
what individual staff can do to support each other
how individuals can help themselves

whole school action

tradition
memorable systems

Memory

long-term memory

- *Pupils' have priorities for using their long-term memory, and we have the same priorities too.*

Pupils draw on their long-term memory to inform them about matters of prime importance. Their priorities for the use of long-term memory are reflected in this publication. Academic learning is necessarily a lower priority for deploying long-term memory than matters of their personal safety, their standing, success and so on. When the priorities are reasonably under control, pupils' long-term memory can gradually be released to focus on learning. We know this from our own experience. When we are upset or angry, it is hard to focus on academic work and think logically or creatively.

Memory

building long-term memory

From our second lesson with a class onwards, we can draw on previous positive experiences with pupils as a reminder of our expectations and their achievements in learning and behaviour. Simple ways we can do this include:

- ☞ Draw on previous subject content or learning experience; refer to it "You will recall that..." and provide a brief resume; use questions to elicit key points.

- ☞ Encourage memory recall when the emotional temperature is low. Examinations demand this skill and are well known for causing emotion and stress to rise!

- ☞ Recall with pupils the school's prime purposes and expectations for learning; for academic, vocational, personal and social development.

- ☞ Create a safe community by reducing stress, avoiding the imposition of pressure which pupils feel to be unmanageable.

- ☞ Promote learning by increasing challenge and encouraging the acceptance of pressure which pupils feel to be manageable and within their potential.

- ☞ Remind pupils of school expectations by applying consistently rewards and sanctions for learning and behaviour.

Memory

what managers can do to support staff

As managers we keep in pupils (and colleagues') minds the code of conduct and its application, for example by referring to it regularly and ensuring that it is displayed prominently. When we monitor the application of rewards and sanctions we seek to develop a system that is fair, memorable and easy to apply.

On a very practical level for our colleagues, it is reassuring when we remember to provide follow-up support to staff facing difficulties, especially when we recall their previous successes and accentuate what has gone right.

what individual staff can do to support each other

As individuals we can remind each other what we have done previously to manage behaviour consistently and to apply rewards and sanctions. It is worth recalling with our colleagues' their previous successes even if they are now facing difficulties in tackling behaviour.

As a staff we can contribute to a resource bank of successful ways for handling difficult situations (like *Best behaviour*).

how individual staff can help themselves

Like actors, we can rehearse and memorise quick ways of showing appreciation, reprimanding and getting the focus on learning. We build our confidence when we develop a repertoire of phrases, expressions, gestures, tone of voice which are successful in handling difficult situations.

Memory

tradition

On public occasions, we portray current successes in learning and in conduct with pupils, staff and parents as part of a long-standing, consistent achievement through collaborative effort by members of the school community.

memorable systems

All of us, managers, teaching and non-teaching staff promote the best behaviour by using:

☛ a short, simply-worded code of conduct which is easy to memorise.

☛ consistent application of rewards and sanctions.

☛ efficient systems to support staff in behaviour management.

☛ straightforward systems that help pupils focus on learning.

Motivation

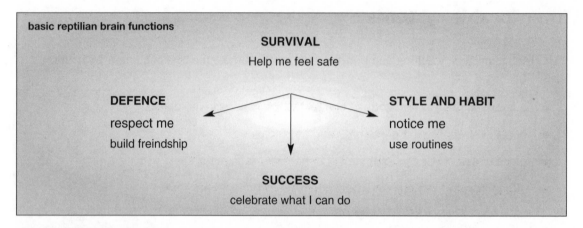

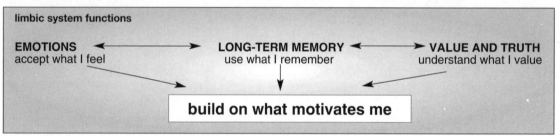

Whether we are pupils, teachers, non-teaching staff or managers, our capacity to behave appropriately, our motivation and our readiness to learn stem from:

1. our reptilian brain functions being satisfied:
- We feel safe
- We feel respected
- We feel we are being given attention
- We have friends, allies, supporters
- We know the routine
- We feel successful

and

2. our brain's limbic system functions being satisfied:
- Our emotions are accepted and engaged
- Our values are understood
- We can use what we remember
- Our memory is free to be used.

When these basic needs are met, our behaviour is at its best and the neo-cortex part of our brain can function at its best too. We are able to work and learn effectively.

Action Points

The following two pages summarise key starting points for effective behaviour management, first for teaching (and non-teaching) staff and then for senior and middle managers.

All the strategies in *Best behaviour* are drawn from successful practice across many schools. Their appearance here is not unlike the advice and recommendations of a fire prevention manual. The implementation of these action points has been found to make a positive long-term contribution to improvement in behaviour in schools.

Unfortunately, a fire prevention manual is not much use when a building is ablaze. Then, people are more concerned about how to hold the hose! That is why this publication comes with the booklet *Best behaviour FIRST AID*. That booklet has different kinds of action points to help cope with difficult behaviour in the heat of the moment.

School staff and managers need both approaches to behaviour management - the longer term and the immediate. Here, both sets of strategies are underpinned by a single rationale about how the human brain works and the recognition that the brains of all of us in the school community have in common functions and needs. The aim is to offer straightforward action points that manage behaviour and promote learning.

BEST BEHAVIOUR

Staff action points

action to meet basic reptilian brain needs

a sense of security
- use classroom layout and organisation systems to foster a sense of security
- organise lessons so that they have a clear structure, an established start and finish
- make our expectations consistent over time, consistent with other staff
- have a few tried and tested strategies for coping with challenging behaviour

respect
- show pupils we value them as people as well as learners
- use a variety of ways to show pupils we value their work
- separate difficult behaviour from the person and criticise the behaviour
- trust colleagues when they offer support and advice

attention
- get to know pupils as individuals and provide positive, supportive attention
- transfer focus away from challenging behaviour and back onto learning
- do not take good work and behaviour for granted; recognise and reward them
- give responsibility to give and gain attention

friendship
- be welcoming, friendly and interested
- admit mistakes, use 'I' messages and be ready to apologise
- encourage dialogue about the learning process
- help pupils relax and grow in confidence in their learning

routine
- teach pupils some routines to help the smooth running and completion of a lesson
- use routine ways of stating planned learning outcomes and task specifications
- reinforce routines to promote consistent expectations
- have a repertoire of routines to help us respond to difficult behaviour

success
- show commitment to pupils as people and learners
- adopt a coaching approach: celebrate success, analyse difficulty, provide support
- take a positive view of ourselves, our pupils and our colleagues
- avoid overlooking achievement and success where we have come to expect it

action to meet the brain's limbic system needs

emotions
- help pupils to use emotions to enrich and strengthen their learning
- provide outlets that allow emotional pressure to be released
- model ways of handling emotions, eg: by using 'I' messages

values
- handle with care other people's values; reinforce shared values
- acknowledge behaviour that accords with the code of conduct
- be alert to prevalent pupil values and those who lead opinion

memory
- draw on previous positive experiences with pupils as a reminder of expectations
- encourage pupils' memory recall
- memorise ways we can show appreciation, reprimand, get the focus onto learning

motivation
- use emotional engagement, relevance and previous success to help motivate

Management action points

action to meet basic reptilian brain needs

a sense of security
- clarify boundaries and appropriate responses when boundaries are crossed
- create differentiated schemes of work
- arrange behaviour management support during lessons
- monitor the effectiveness of policies and procedures for safety and security

respect
- model respect in our dealings with colleagues and pupils
- ensure that existing groups have real influence and responsibility
- build a culture of respect, acknowledge achievements, link with the community
- check how incidents are being handled

attention
- give supportive attention to staff colleagues and to pupils
- hear, understand, notice and appreciate all in the school community
- involve staff, pupils and parents in some aspects of running the school
- promote equal opportunities

friendship
- instigate positive discussion about the occurrence of difficult behaviour
- check what is promoting or hindering friendly interaction, politeness and concern
- introduce a buddy system
- place pupils into tutor groups with sensitivity about existing friendship circles

routine
- create department routines that overcome difficulties in classroom management
- provide support to colleagues to prepare for and debrief difficult lessons
- establish routine procedures for handling difficult behaviour
- foster staff use of a repertoire of routines to help them respond to difficult behaviour

success
- know what staff are doing; give recognition to their strengths and successes
- use career development opportunities to reward staff successes
- link a personal and professional development programme to appraisal
- help the whole school community view itself positively

action to meet the brain's limbic system needs

emotions
- enable staff to express emotions about their work with pupils, colleagues and us
- show that we do listen to and reflect upon concerns
- use assemblies, special events, the arts to express emotions

values
- check how whole-school values apply to and affect behaviour management
- express whole-school values simply and publish them
- update agreement on whole-school values by all sections of the school community

memory
- refer to and apply the code of conduct regularly
- portray current successes as part of long-standing, consistent achievement
- create simple, easily remembered, efficient systems for behaviour management

motivation
- show staff and pupils that we value them, their commitment and achievements

Index

Network Educational Press Publications

THE SCHOOL EFFECTIVENESS SERIES

Best behaviour is the ninth title in The School Effectiveness Series, which focuses on practical and useful ideas for school teachers. This series addresses the issues of whole school improvement, explores new knowledge about teaching and learning, and offers straightforward solutions which teachers can use to make life more rewarding for themselves and those they teach.

Book 1: *Accelerated Learning in the Classroom* by Alistair Smith
ISBN: 1-85539-034-5

- The first book in the UK to apply new knowledge about the brain to classroom practice
- Contains practical methods so teachers can apply accelerated learning theories to their own classrooms
- Aims to increase the pace of learning and deepen understanding
- Includes advice on how to create the ideal environment for learning and how to help learners fulfil their potential
- Full of lively illustrations, diagrams and plans
- Offers practical solutions on improving performance, motivation and understanding
- Contains a checklist of action points for the classroom - 21 ways to improve learning

Book 2: *Effective Learning Activities* by Chris Dickinson
ISBN: 1-85539-035-3

- An essential teaching guide which focuses on practical activities to improve learning
- Aims to improve results through effective learning, which will raise achievement, deepen understanding, promote self-esteem and improve motivation
- Includes activities which are designed to promote differentiation and understanding
- Offers advice on how to maximise the use of available - and limited - resources
- Includes activities suitable for GCSE, National Curriculum, Highers, GSVQ and GNVQ
- From the author of the highly acclaimed Differentiation: A Practical Handbook of Classroom Strategies

Book 3: *Effective Heads of Department* by Phil Jones & Nick Sparks
ISBN: 1-85539-036-1

- An ideal support for Heads of Department looking to develop necessary management skills
- Contains a range of practical systems and approaches; each of the eight sections ends with a "checklist for action"
- Designed to develop practice in line with OFSTED expectations and DfEE thinking by monitoring and improving quality
- Addressees issues such as managing resources, leadership, learning, departmental planning and making assessment valuable
- Includes useful information for Senior Managers in schools who are looking to enhance the effectiveness of their Heads of Department

Book 4: *Lessons are for Learning* by Mike Hughes
ISBN: 1-85539-038-8

- Brings together the theory of learning with the realities of the classroom environment
- Encourages teachers to reflect on their own classroom practice and challenges them to think about why they teach in the way they do
- Develops a clear picture of what constitutes effective classroom practice
- Offers practical suggestions for activities that bridge the gap between recent developments in the theory of learning and the constraints of classroom teaching
- Ideal for stimulating thought and generating discussion
- Written by a practising teacher who has also worked as a teaching advisor, a PGCE co-coordinator and an OFSTED inspector

Book 5: *Effective Learning in Science* by Paul Denley and Keith Bishop
ISBN: 1-85539-039-6
- A new book that looks at planning for effective learning within the context of science
- Encourages discussion about the aims and purposes in teaching science and the role of subject knowledge in effective teaching
- Tackles issues such as planning for effective learning, the use of resources and other relevant management issues
- Offers help in development of a departmental plan to revise schemes of work, resources, classroom strategies, in order to make learning and teaching more effective
- Ideal for any science department aiming to increase performance and improve results

Book 6: *Raising boys' Achievement* by Jon Pickering
ISBN: 1-85539-040-X
- Addresses the causes of boys' underachievement and offers possible solutions
- Focuses the search for causes and solutions on teachers working in the classroom
- Looks at examples of good practice in schools to help guide the planning and implementation of strategies to raise achievement
- Offers practical , 'real' solutions, along with tried and tested training suggestions
- Ideal as a basis for INSET or as a guide to practical activities for classroom teachers

Book 7: *Effective Provision for Able & Talented Children* by Barry Price
ISBN: 1-85539-041-8
- Basic theory, necessary procedures and turning theory into practice
- Main methods of identifying the able and talented
- Concerns about achievement and appropriate strategies to raise achievement
- The role of the classroom teacher, monitoring and evaluation techniques
- Practical enrichment activities and appropriate resources

Book 8: *Effective Careers Education & Guidance* by Andrew Edwards and Anthony Barnes
ISBN: 1-85539-045-0
- Strategic planning of the careers programme as part of the wider curriculum
- Practical consideration of managing careers education and guidance
- Practical activities for reflection and personal learning, and case studies where such activities have been used
- Aspects of guidance and counselling involved in helping students to understand their won capabilities and form career plans
- Strategies for reviewing and developing existing practice

Book 10: *The Effective School Governor* by David Marriott
ISBN: 1-85539-042-6
Straightforward guidance on how to fulfil a governor's role and responsibilities
Develops your personal effectiveness as an individual governor
Practical support on how to be an effective member of the governing team
Audio tape for use in car or at home

Book 11: *Improving Personal Effectiveness for Managers in Schools by James Johnson*
ISBN: 1-85539-049-3
- An invaluable resource for new and experienced teachers in both primary and secondary schools
- Contains practical strategies for improving leadership and management skills
- Focuses on self-management skills, managing difficult situations, working under pressure, developing confidence, creating a team ethos and communicating effectively

Book 12: *Making Pupil Data Powerful by Maggie Pringle and Tony Cobb*
ISBN: 1-85539-053-3

- Shows teachers in primary, middle and secondary schools how to interpret pupils' performance data and how to use it to enhance teaching and learning
- Provides practical advice on analysing performance and learning behaviours, measuring progress, predicting future attainment, setting targets and ensuring continuity and progression
- Explains how to interpret national initiatives on data-analysis, benchmarking and target-setting, and to ensure that these have value in the classroom

Book 13: *Closing the Learning Gap by Mike Hughes*
ISBN: 1-85539-051-5

- Help teachers, departments and schools to close the Learning Gap between what we know about effective learning and what actually goes in the classroom
- Encourages teachers to reflect on ways in which they teach, and to identify and implement strategies for improving their practice
- Full of practical advice and real, tested strategies for improvement
- Written by a teacher, for teachers, to stimulate thought and interest 'at a glance'

Book 14: *Getting Started by Henry Liebling*
ISBN: 1-85539-054-X

- An induction guide for newly qualified teachers giving advice on their first year of teaching- how to get to know the school and their new pupils, how to work with their induction tutor and when to ask for help
- Includes masses of practical advice on issues such as getting to grips with the school's documentation, managing pupils' behaviour, time management, classroom management and dealing with tiredness and stress
- Draws on the author's extensive experience as a lecturer and teacher trainer
  Gives NQTs guidance on what to look for when observing experienced colleagues, how to evaluate and develop their own teaching, and to build on their Career Entry Profile to meet the requirements of the induction standards
- Provides an overview of theories in teaching and learning styles, models of teaching, and teaching and learning strategies

OTHER PUBLICATIONS

Imagine that... by Stephen Bowkett
    ISBN: 1-85539-043-4
- Hands on, user-friendly manual for stimulating creative thinking, talking and writing in the classroom
- Provides over 100 practical and immediately useable classroom activities and games that can be used in isolation, or in combination, to help meet the requirements and standards of the National Curriculum
- Explores the nature of creative thinking and how this can be effectively driven through an ethos of positive encouragement, mutual support and celebration of success and achievement
- Empowers children to learn and how to learn

Helping with Reading by Anne Butterworth and Angela White
    ISBN: 1-95539-044-2
- Includes sections on 'Hearing Children Read'. 'Word Recognition' and 'Phonics'
- Provides precisely focused, easily implemented follow-up activities for pupils who need extra reinforcement of basic reading skills
- Activities which directly relate to the National Curriculum and 'Literacy Hour' group work. They are clear, practical and easily implemented. Ideas and activities can also be incorporated into Individual Education Plans.
- Aims to address current concerns about reading standards and to provide support in view of the growing use of classroom assistants and parents to help with the teaching of reading

Self Intelligence by Stephen Bowkett
    ISBN: 1-85539-055-8
- Designed to help explore and develop emotional resourcesfulness in yourself and the children you teach
- High self-esteem underpins success in education. More broadly, emotionaly resourcefulness results in improved behaviour and higher standards.

Effective Resources for Able and Talented Children by Barry Teare
    ISBN: 1-85539-050-7
- Sequel to Effective Provisions for Able and Talented Children
- Provides photocopiable resources for Key Stages 2 and 3
- Arranged into 4 themes: Literacy - Mathematics/Numeracy, Science, Hummanities

THE ACCELERATED LEARNING SERIES

Book 1 : *Accelerated Learning in Practice* by Alistair Smith
ISBN: 1-85539-048-5
- The author's second book which takes Nobel Prize winning brain research into the classroom
- Structured to help readers access and retain the information neccessary to begin to accelerate their own learning and that f the students they teach
- Contains over 100 learning tools, case studies from 36 schools and an up to the minute section
- Includes 9 principles of learning based on brain research and the author's 7 Stage Accelerated Learning cycle

Book 2 : *The Alps Approach* by Alistair Smith and Nicola Call
ISBN: 1-85539-056-6
- Takes research collected by Alistair Smith and shows how it can be used to great effect in the primary classroom
- Provides practical and accessible examples of strategies used at a UK primary school where SATs results shot up as a consequence
- Gives readers the opportunity to develop the alps approach for themselves and for children in their care

Book 3 : *Mapwise, Accelerated Learning Through Visible Thinking* by Oliver Caviglioli & Ian Harris
ISBN: 1-85539-059-0
- This book aims at improving thinking skills through teacher explanation and pupil understanding, and so improves your school's capacity for learning
- Makes teacher planning, teaching and reviewing easier and more effective
- Brilliantly illustrated, it offers the most effective means of addressing the National Curriculum thinking skills requirements by infusing thinking into subject teaching.

Multiple Intelligence Posters
A set of 9 clear A2 student posters, covering each of the multiple intelligences as described in 'Accelerated Learning'.

EDUCACTION PERSONNEL MANAGEMENT SERIES

The Well Teacher by Maureen Cooper
management startegies for beating stress, promoting staff health and reducing absence
ISBN: 1-85539-058-2

Gives clear management startegies for promoting staff health, beating stress and reducing staff absence. Stress is not peculiar to staff in education, but is a common cause of absence. Large amounts of limited schools budgets are spent each year on sick pay and supply cover. This book giver straightforward practical advice on how to deal strategically with health issues through practively promoting staff health. It includes suggestions for reducing stress levels in schools. It also outlines how to deal with individual cases of staff absence.

Managing Challenging People by Bev Curtis and Maureen Cooper
delaing with staf conduct
ISBN: 1-85539-057-4

This handbook deals with managing staff whose conduct gives cause for concern. It summarises the employment relationships in schools and those areas of education and employment law relevant to staff discipline. It looks at the difference between conduct and capability, and misconduct and gross misconduct, and describes disciplinary and dimissal procedures relating to teaching and non-teaching staff and headteachers. Throughout the book there are case studies, model procedures and pro-forma letters to help schools with these difficult issues.

Managing poor Performance by Bev Curtis and Maureen Cooper
handling staff capability issues
ISBN: 1-85539-062-0

A school's employees form one of the most important resources in the task of providing a quality education for its pupils. Good people-management skills are crucial in ensuring the effectiveness of staff. When there are problems with capability, the first step is to identify the staff with poor performance. But historically, help in putting things right has been limited.

Managing Poor Performance, explains clearly why capability is important, and gives advice on how to identify staff with poor performance and how to help them improve. It outlines the legal position and the role of governors, an details the various stages of formal capability procedures and dismissal hearings. The book provides model letters to use and is illustrated by real-life case studies. This provides the help you need to give you confidence in tackling these difficult issues.